The Art Of
LOGGING OUT

www.booksbyboxer.com

Published in the UK by
Books By Boxer, Leeds, LS13 4BS
© Books By Boxer 2018
All Rights Reserved

ISBN: 9781909732612

FOREWORD

The art of logging out is to use your valuable poo time to switch off from the daily grind and relax with a book, ideally full of fun, interesting and useless facts like this one.

As you luxuriate in your sanctuary, safe in your quiet space behind the bathroom door reading your book, your woes and troubles will be temporarily suspended, work and worries whisked away, enabling you to complete the business at hand in peace and tranquillity.

As science writer Ferris Jabr recently said in *Scientific American*, "downtime replenishes the brain's stores of attention and motivation… and is essential to both achieve our highest levels of performance and simply form stable memories in everyday life".

What he didn't say was:
Take your time to do your poo,
Ignore the world outside the loo,
You'll come out keen, a real go-getter
And smash your problems much more better.

Are you sitting **comfortably?**

At **peace** with the **world?**

Door **locked?**

Then it's **time** to begin...

logging out!

Things To **Wonder** About...

Time Thinking

- If it wasn't for the last minute, would anything ever get done?

- Why is it that when your plane is late, the one you want to transfer to is on time? And vice versa.

- Can you fritter away anything else but time?

Theological Relief

- If God dropped acid, would he see people?

- Did the bishop say anything back to the actress?

- If God really existed, how come he allowed a film like Pearl Harbour to be made?

- Who does the Pope go to for confession?

- Is man one of God's blunders or is God one of man's?

- Did St. Paul ever get any replies to all those letters he wrote to the Corinthians?

- If God really wanted us to decimalise, why weren't there ten apostles instead of twelve?

- Why are angels never allowed to sit down in heaven?

- How coincidental it was that Jesus was born on Christmas morning?

- Who created God?

- How many more witnesses do they need before Jehovah's trial starts?

- Was it the apple on the tree that got Adam and Eve kicked out of the Garden of Eden or the pair on the ground?

- Where do sick people from Lourdes go to be cured?

- If power corrupts and absolute power corrupts absolutely, where does that leave God?

- If man is dust, as the Bible tells us, why do we not get muddy in the rain?

- Is a religious awakening something that happens to a congregation after a boring sermon?

- If we're all made in God's image, why don't I have a flowing white beard and a more forgiving attitude?

- If we all came from Adam and Eve, is the whole population of the world not the product of an incestuous relationship?

- If liars don't get to heaven, as the priest who taught me religion always insisted, is there anyone up there besides George Washington?

- If there's going to be weeping and gnashing of teeth on the Last Day, how will this affect those wearing dentures?

- In the event of a miracle, who do atheists thank?

- Why should we worship Jesus when his name is a swear word?

- If God has been around forever, what did He do before creating the world?

- Considering Jesus was a Jew, how come he's got a Mexican name?

- If God got amnesia, would he become an agnostic?

- If God is the answer, what's the question?

- Why were born-again Christians born in the first place?

- Is atheism a non-prophet making organisation?

- If heaven is invisible, why did God put a wall and gate round it?

- Was Eve the only woman who ever took a man's side?

- If God really exists, why didn't he put wrinkles on people's bums instead of their faces?

- What do you say to God when He sneezes?

- If you're born again, does your mother feel the pain?

- Why did God spend six whole days making the world when he knew how lousy it was going to turn out?

- How is it that religion is usually alive and well in countries where the people aren't?

- Who do atheists scream to when they're having sex?

- Who do atheists thank when it's a fine day?

- If we've been put on the earth to help others, as the Bible tells us, what are others here for?

- Why is it that people who believe in reincarnation were always kings or emperors in their previous lives? Why are there not any reincarnated beggars around?

- What if there HAD been room at the inn?

- If we're all God's children, what's so special about Jesus?

- What if Jesus had been a girl?

- If God meant us to be happy, why does he allow long lost relatives to visit us at Christmas?

- Apart from the known and the unknown, what else is there?

- Could God make a square circle?

- Can atheists get insurance for an act of God?

- Did Noah have woodpeckers and woodworms on the ark? How did he not sink?

- In libraries, do they put the bible in the fiction or non-fiction section?

Procreational Contemplation

- Why do we say 90% of accidents are caused by children when the reality of the situation is that 90% of children are caused by accident?

- If Dolly Parton had triplets, considering my luck is so bad, would I be the one on the bottle?

- Do adults ask their children what they want to be when they grow up mainly because they're looking for ideas?

People Pontification

- If people talk bullshit, would nonsensical bulls talk peopleshit?

- Why can you never see people who owe you money, whereas people you owe money to are EVERYWHERE?

- Is there such a thing as the beginning of your tether?

- Why do people say sorry when YOU step on THEIR toe?

- Why do people always die in alphabetical order?

- How is it that most of the people who really know how to run the country are either driving taxis or cutting hair?

- Why do people say 'To make a long story short' when all they're really doing is adding six words to it?

- If Superman is so smart, why does he wear his underpants outside his pants?

- Why do women wear micro-mini skirts and then spend half their time pulling them down?

- Why is it that when we whisper something, people deem it to be of the utmost importance?

- Why do snorers always go to sleep first?

- Where do people in hell tell their enemies to go?

- Why do we call it a one night stand when people are doing anything but standing?

- If it wasn't for half the people in the world, would the other half be all of them?

- Is enough being done for the apathetic?

- Why can't people describe spiral staircases without using their hands?

- Why do people buy things they don't need with money they don't have to impress people they don't like?

- How was William Holden able to tell the story of his life in Sunset Boulevard after being shot dead?

- Do people who come out of comas feel really rested?

- When you tell people you've mislaid something, why do they say, 'Where did you lose it?' How can you answer that?

Historical Hypothesis

- Why did Shakespeare use so many quotations in his books?

- If Helen of Troy's face could really launch a thousand ships, why do they waste all that champagne?

- Could Karl Marx's grave be said to be a communist plot?

- When people asked George Washington for his ID, did he just pull out a quarter?

- If Bacon wrote Shakespeare, who wrote Bacon?

Drinking Deliberations

- If the pub bouncer gets drunk, who throws him out?

- Are people who drink and drive putting the quart before the hearse?

- Do pink elephants see PEOPLE when they get drunk?

- If sighted people see double with excess alcohol, why don't blind people see single?

- Is staying drunk the best way to avoid hangovers?

- If booze is the answer, what's the question?

- Why do you see more old drunks alive than old doctors?

- How can you still be thirsty after a night of gross over-indulgence in alcohol?

- How is it that drunks know the answer to the world's problems, but not their way home?

- Why is it called Alcoholics Anonymous when the first thing you do upon joining it is tell everyone your name?

- If there were pubs on the moon, would they have atmosphere?

- Could the person who set up Alcoholics Anonymous be described as a pioneer even if he drank a lot?

- Why do we drink to forget, but drink so much we eventually can't remember what it was we were trying to forget.

Healthy Consideration

- Why is belly button fluff the same no matter what colour clothes you're wearing?

- Is acupuncture any good for pins and needles?

- Why do people order Big Macs with a large helping of French fries and then go for diet coke?

- Why do appetisers usually make me LOSE my appetite?

- Should psychiatrists charge double for treating schizophrenics?

- Why do gynaecologists leave the room while their patients are undressing?

- Is circumcision a bloody rip-off?

- Why do we wash our faces in hot water and our teeth in cold water?

- Considering blind people wear sunglasses, why don't deaf people wear earmuffs?

- Why can't snorers ever hear themselves snore?

- Why are reminders always salutary?

- Why do fat people never get anorexia?

- If vegetarians only eat vegetables, why do humanitarians not eat humans?

- Why are orthodontists not called orthodentists?

- Why can we always read a doctor's bill, but never their prescriptions?

- Why can I never get the pain at the doctor's?

- Why don't hospitals have the intensive care unit closer to the cashier's office?

- Why do people who work in health shops always look so unhealthy?

- Why did people take acid in the 1960s to make the world look weird, and now that it IS weird they take Prozac to try and make it look normal?

- Why do they keep the back pain medicine on the bottom shelf at the pharmacy?

- Is a psychiatrist called a shrink because that's what he does to your wallet?

- Why do doctors always have signatures that look like cardiographs?

Travel Trepidations

- If the world is indeed finite, as scientists suggest, why do my odd socks never turn up anywhere?

- Why do we call it rush hour when traffic is at a standstill?

- Is a Mexican Wave in Mexico just a wave?

- How is it that road maps tell you absolutely everything… except how to fold them?

- Are articulated trucks better at expressing themselves than ordinary ones?

Political Pondering

- If all the world's a stage, and all the men and women merely players, where does the audience come from?

- Should those who oppose freedom of speech be silenced?

- Why do politicians have to stand in an election to get a seat?

Money Musings

- Why do creditors have better memories then debtors?

- Why should we do anything for posterity when posterity has done damn all for us?

- If rich people asked poor people to die for them for a fee, would poor people then make a great living?

- Is money the only nice thing about rich people?

- If money doesn't grow on trees, why do banks have branches?

Animal Antics

- Why don't sheep shrink in wet weather?

- If dogs are a man's best friend and diamonds are a girl's, why don't dogs and diamonds set up house together and save the world a fortune on alimony and bitter splits?

- Why are animals made of meat if we're not supposed to eat them?

- Why do cats have pyjamas and bees have knees?

- Do bees hum because they don't know the words?

- Considering that toast always falls on its buttered side and a cat on its feet, if you superglued a cat to the unbuttered side of a slice of toast, what would happen?

- If owls are so wise, why don't they get off the night shift?

- Do sheep count people to get to sleep?

- Why are guinea pigs called what they are when they're not pigs and don't come from Guinea?

- How will I know if my goldfish is incontinent?

- Accepting the fact that curiosity killed the cat, what exactly was the cat curious about?

- Why do we think it's horrible when animals kill humans but not when humans kill animals?

Movie Meanderings

- Why is it that whenever a movie character turns on the TV, there's always a programme on that relates directly to them?

- Why do maidens in distress always go up creepy stairs in films at the dead of night when they hear suspicious noises, instead of legging it out of the house altogether?

- Does television destroy the art of conversation or is it the other way round?

- Why do characters in films never seem to have to go to the toilet?

- Why do trailers precede films?

- How is it that whenever they want a taxi, one inevitably appears?

- Why do heroes feel an irresistible urge to sneeze just at the moment the villain is passing by where they're hiding?

- If we're to really believe women when they say the thing they want most in a man is a sense of humour, why didn't Angelina Jolie date Woody Allen instead of Brad Pitt?

- Why is it only suspended cops in films that can crack cases?

- Why is it that the villains in films today have to be killed about eight times before they finally die?

- Why is it that during movie car chases on dangerous cliffs, the driver never uses the rear view mirror to check on the villain pursuing him, preferring to risk his life by looking behind him?

- Why is it that only people who live on craggy mountainsides in films get their car brakes booby trapped?

- Why do movie heroes' bullets always reach their targets, but never movie villains' ones?

- Did ET go home because he got the phone bill?

- If violence on TV causes violence on the streets, as we're told, then why doesn't comedy on the TV cause comedy on the streets?

- Why do people in films always have the exact change for everything?

- Why do movie cop heroes always have drink problem's, bad marriages, and hair-trigger tempers that land them in trouble with their superiors?

Why Worry?

• Are rooms always at room temperature?

• Where do ice cream vans go in winter?

• Why is there always one spoon left in the sink
  after you've finished the washing up?

• Why do floorboards only creak after midnight?

• Is it now all right to cry over spilt milk, considering
  it's so expensive these days?

No Answer

- If cannibals don't like their mothers-in-law, can they leave them at the side of the plate?

- Why do men have nipples?

- Has modern music gone totally to yell?

- Should so-called open minds be closed for repairs?

- Considering the state of the world, could Nostradamus now be seen as an optimist?

- Is the best way to save face to keep the lower half of it shut?

- Why do I keep seeing documentaries about TV being bad for me on TV?

- Why are camouflage jackets so conspicuous?

Drive Mad

- Why do otherwise sane people do the things they do when driving round roundabouts?

- Why is it that when a car is causing an obstruction, they clamp it and leave it there?

- On public transport, why is it always more interesting to read other people's newspapers than your own one?

- Could you avoid road accidents by driving on the pavement?

- Why do people leave cars worth thousands of pounds in the driveway and lock all their junk in the garage?

- Why is the first person at the traffic lights always the last to see them change from red to green?

- Why are car dashboards called that when they don't go any faster than the rest of the car?

- If 30% of car accidents are caused by alcohol, does that mean teetotallers are responsible for the other 70%?

- Do driving instructors ever give crash courses?

Love Dup

- Is love the worst four-lettered word of all?

- Is it easier to lie with a straight face or a curved body?

- Why do people praise marriage because it's an institution? Who wants to live in an institution?

- If music is the food of love, why aren't more rabbits born playing the banjo?

- Is a honeymoon the mourning after the knot before?

- If you left your heart in San Francisco, would you be the first living donor?

- If sex is supposed to be natural, why are there so many books on how to do it?

- If love is blind, why is lingerie so popular?

- Is the best way to approach a woman with a past - with a present?

- Why do women wait until they've been kissed by a man before they slap him?

- Why are women who play 'hard to get' usually hard to take?

- How does an insomniac meet the girl of his dreams?

- If love is blind, why are so many men attracted to beautiful women?

Out There

- Why does opportunity always seem to knock at the most inopportune moment?

- Do people who ask you for advice really only seem to want corroboration?

- Did Oliver Hardy spend too much time resting on his Laurel?

- Has an arrested mime artist the right to remain silent?

- Why can't we tickle ourselves?

- Why does 'manslaughter' sound much worse than murder?

- How do they get the coating to stick on a non-stick frying pan?

- Why do people who say 'Unaccustomed as I am to public speaking' always insist on proving it?

- If ignorance is really bliss, why aren't more of my friends happy?

- Why does grass only smell after you cut it?

- Why do petrol station owners lock their toilets? Are they afraid someone will steal them?

- Why does the sun darken your skin but make your hair lighter?

- Why can't we keep our eyes open when we sneeze?

- Considering most accidents occur five minutes from home, why don't people move house?

Life's Answers

- How do blind people dream?

- Is a tortoise with no shell naked or homeless?

- Why is 'below par' a good thing when you're talking about golf but bad when you're talking about your work performance?

- How do you know when you've run out of invisible ink?

- Why does the word 'monosyllabic' have five syllables?

- Why is it so hard to remember how to spell 'mnemonic'?

- Can you wear a beret back to front?

- If a word is mis-spelled in the dictionary, how will we know?

- If Barbie is so popular, why do we have to buy her friends?

- Why do psychics divorce – can they not see it coming?

- Would a condemned man who asked for a cigarette as a last wish be refused one because they're bad for your health?

- What should people take for kleptomania?

- Why do we only ever hear of figments in relation to the imagination? Are there no other kinds of figments?

- Why do phone cords get so tangled?

- Should you use a silencer if you shoot a mime artist?

- Why do answerphone messages usually start with the words 'I can't come to the phone right now?' If they could, there wouldn't be any need for a message.

- Why do British people sound American when they sing?

Lucid Moments

- If we live in a society of free speech, as we're told, why are there phone bills?

- Where do laps go when people stand up?

- Why does it always take longer to get somewhere than it does to come back?

- Why are care-givers and caretakers basically the same thing?

- If you go to enough evening classes, could you learn to be an evening?

- If a little knowledge is a dangerous thing, how much do you need to be out of danger?

- How can you have an amicable divorce? If you're amicable, why get divorced?

- How do writers get material for biographies of recluses?

- When you lose something, why do people say, 'It's always the last place you look.' If it wasn't, you'd have stopped looking.

- Why do the Dutch people have two words for their country – Holland and the Netherlands – neither of which contains the word 'Dutch'?

- After eating, do amphibians have to wait an hour before getting out of the water?

- What happens to the hole when the cheese is gone?

- Does expecting the unexpected not make the unexpected the expected?

- Did Bo Peep do it for the insurance?

- Why does your mother tell you to wear clean underwear in case of an accident? If a car knocks you down, they won't be clean for long.

- Why are there so many more agony aunts than agony uncles?

- What do you do with the problem solvers after the problems are solved?

- Why do alarms go off instead of on?

- Whose bicycle pump did Dunlop borrow to blow up the first pneumatic tyre?

- Do Eskimos have to ensure their homes against fire?

- Why isn't there another word for thesaurus?

- Why do people who are retiring (i.e. entering a phase of their life when punctuality isn't of the essence) usually get watches as presents?

Uncommon Sense

- If your nose runs and your feet smell, would you not be upside down?

- Why do movie characters with terminal illnesses usually look better than the rest of the cast?

- If nothing acts faster than Anadin, why don't people take nothing for their headaches?

- Who do the Joneses keep up with?

- Why are there no husband-swapping parties?

- Why do places that ban smoking have smoke alarms?

- Why is there only one Monopolies commission?

- Is sexual harassment a problem for the self employed?

- Is nostalgia a thing of the past?

- If you went back in time and took this page with you, could you read it before I wrote it?

- Why do people feel it necessary to nail down the lid of coffins?

- Why is there snow on the tops of mountains when they're nearer the sun than the bottom of them?

- Why at parties, do people keep asking you where you work, but at work people rarely ask you what parties you go to?

- Why doesn't the word 'phonetic' sound the way it's spelt?

- How do painkillers know where the pain is?

- If practice makes perfect and nobody's perfect, why practise?

- Why do machines always break down the week after the guarantee runs out?

- Was Humpty Dumpty pushed?

- Why are jokes called double-meaning when they really only have one meaning?

- How does Bono manage to comb his hair without scratching his halo?

- If rhino horn is such a powerful aphrodisiac, why are rhinos an endangered species?

- Considering lawyers are disbarred and clergymen defrocked, should pigs not be disgruntled, electricians delighted, musicians denoted and cowboys deranged?

- Are egotists always me-deep in conversation?

- Why do overlook and oversee mean opposite things?

- Why do you always get itchy in that part of your back that's too low to reach by going over your shoulder with your hand, and too high to reach up to round your waist?

- If there was a hospital strike, would they use a skeleton staff?

- What was the man who first realised cows produced milk from their teats doing at the time he discovered that fact.

- Did Michael Jackson have any original bits left in his body?

- Why does food always taste better at a picnic?

- Why do politicians always talk about dying for their country but never of killing for it?

- How long will the meek be able to hold onto the earth after they inherit it?

- Why is Larry always so happy?

- Can you have an uneven keel?

- Did Elgin die with all his marbles?

Farside Frolicking

- Does the bear pray? Does the Pope poop in the woods?

- Is life an incurable disease?

- Is the best way to get over a man to get under another one?

- Why is it called the tourist season if we can't shoot them?

- If your parents didn't have any children, does that mean you won't either?

- Would crime still pay if the Government ran it?

- If you think before you speak, will the other fellow get in his gag first?

- Is a pas de deux the father of twins?

- Are the best things in life duty-free?

- Why do the wrong people suffer from inferiority complexes?

- Is the pun the lowest form of wit only if you didn't think of it first?

- If we saw ourselves as the neighbours did, would we move?

- Do philosophers seem to have a problem for every solution?

- Does life really have to have a meaning? Could it not be like one of those old French movies?

- Do feminist cornflakes go snap, crackle and mum?

- Is there anything more annoying in life than not being invited to a party you wouldn't be seen dead at?

- Why do New Year resolutions usually get broken by January 2nd?

- How is it that in marriage one plus one equals three?

- Why do mothers feed the hand that bites them?

- Are children more difficult to bear after birth than before?

- Why do bachelors never take yes for an answer?

- Do nudists suffer from clothestrophobia?

- If evolution really worked, would we not have more than one pair of hands?

- If Mary did indeed have a little lamb, who would the father be?

- Is the use of French phrases passé?

- Why do experts take what you already know and make it sound confusing?

- Is it not true that you CAN burn the candle at both ends if you just cut off a bit of the bottom to find the wick?

- What was the best thing before sliced bread?

- Is the expression 'tired old cliche' a tired old cliche?

- Why do people conceal names to protect the innocent? Surely it's the guilty who need protection. What have the innocent to hide?

- Can you do anything with your thumbs but twiddle them?

- What did my creative writing teacher mean when he said, 'Be obscure clearly'?

- Why don't fortune tellers ever win the Lotto?

- How do centipedes learn to walk?

- If you bought one of those anti-smoking tapes you play when you're asleep, would they stop you smoking when you woke up as well?

- What's the birth rate like on the Virgin Islands?

- If the brain was simple enough for us to understand, would we be too simple to understand it?

- How did they measure hailstones before golf balls were invented?

- Did Superboy wear his nappies over his romper suit?

- If four out of five people in the world suffer from diarrhoea, does that mean the fifth one actually enjoys it?

Sublime Ridiculity

- Are there no Preparations from A to G?

- If quizzes are quizzical, what are tests?

- How do people who drive snow-ploughs get to work?

- How could the world have begun with a big bang when there had to be something before that to MAKE the bang?

- Why does Christmas always come just when the shops are so busy?

- Would lightning be faster if it didn't have that bend in it?

- If a single bed is three feet wide, why is a double one only 4 feet 6 inches?

- Before drawing boards were invented, what did people go back to when they made a mistake?

- Did Pandora own anything else besides a box?

- Why do solicitors prepare statements of up to a thousand pages and still persist in calling them 'briefs'?

- If God intended us to be naturists, would we not have been born that way?

- Do they sterilise needles before lethal injections?

- Why do unwatched pots boil immediately?

- Why are they called apartments when they're all stuck together?

- Why does sour cream have a sell-by date?

- If Elvis is really packing shelves down in my local supermarket, (as people keep telling me) how is it that I never see him?

- When you visit psychics, why do they have to ask you your name?

- Why do people believe in a supernatural being they've never seen?

- How is Tarzan clean-shaven?

- If rocket scientists are so smart, why do they count backwards?

- How do you find the people involved in subliminal advertising?

Unanswered Answers

- How does the government know if people have returned their census forms?

- If Queen Elizabeth wrote a book, would she be given royalties?

- Apart from the known and the unknown, what else is there?

- Why do country & western singers get so cut up about dead dogs?

- Why do so many bald people have beards – are they trying to prove something?

- Why do they put bath taps exactly at the place you're likely to bonk your head?

- Why doesn't somebody invent a razor that can get at that awkward little bit in the middle of your upper lip?

- Is there another word for synonym?

- Considering high-fat milk is bad for you, why don't more cows get heart attacks?

- If atoms are empty spaces, as we're told, and most matter is composed of atoms, why can't I walk through walls?

- How is it that there's just enough news in the paper every day to fill it?

- Why is the winner of Miss Universe always from Earth?

- If you put a coffee table in your bedroom would it keep you awake at night?

- Why did kamikaze pilots wear helmets?

- What happens to furniture that's too old for the poor and not yet old enough for the rich?

- Why don't moths come out in the day if they like light so much?

- Do fish have to rest for an hour after eating before they swim?

- Why is there no ham in hamburgers?

- Why, despite the cost of living, is it still so popular?

- Is it progress if a cannibal uses a knife and fork?

- Will shop assistants one day stop acting like they're doing me a favour by serving me?

- Could voyeurs be called guilty bystanders?

- How is it that so many people in Who's Who haven't a clue what's what?

- Are hefty books about the preservation of rain forests counterproductive?

- Why do we kill people who kill people to show that killing people is wrong?

- Why is common sense so uncommon?

Ex-box Thinking

- At a nudist wedding where do you keep the rings?

- What do gardeners do when they retire?

- Where do the homeless have 90% of their accidents?

- What colour hair do they put on the driving licences of bald men?

- Why is a bra singular but knickers plural?

- Do DJs work for the love of mike?

- How can you have a peace-keeping 'force'?

- If the formula for water is H20, is the one for ice H20 squared?

- Why are there disabled parking places in front of skating rinks?

- Is innuendo a Greek suppository?

- Would an egoist's suicide be called a crime of passion?

- If someone who can't count finds a four-leaf clover, is he entitled to all the good luck it entails?

- Where do nudists keep their keys to the nudist colony?

- At the AGM of the National Clairvoyants Association, do they read out NEXT year's minutes?

- Do illiterate people enjoy alphabet soup?

- Why is it that if you blow in a dog's face he gets mad at you, but if you take him for a spin in the car, the first thing he does is put his head out the window?

- Was Caesar born by Caesarean section?

- Is French kissing in France just called kissing?

- Why is it that nobody cares if a banker writes a bad poem, but if a poet writes a bad cheque he ends up in jail?

- Why is a fat chance and a slim chance the same thing?

- Did the first man who ever looked in a mirror recognise himself?

- How do amnesia victims remember how to talk?

- If you own a piece of land, do you own it all the way to the core of the earth?

- Why do ideas that seem astoundingly bright on a Saturday night after a few beers become screamingly dull in the cold light of Sunday morning?

- What would a world without hypothetical situations be like?

- How is it that mineral water that has 'trickled through the mountains for centuries' has a sell-by date?

- Is a friend in need a bloody nuisance?

- Why do toasters have a setting that burns the bread to a frazzle?

- What do people in China call their good plates?

- If a man who plays the piano is called a pianist, why is a person who drives a racing car not called a racist?

- When cheese gets its picture taken, what does it say?

- How will I know when I'm enlightened?

- If it's natural to kill, why do men have to go into training to learn how to do it?

- Can you have a chip anywhere else but on your shoulder?

- How do they put up 'Keep Off the Grass' signs?

- Do infants enjoy infancy as much as adults enjoy adultery?

- Why are there playwrights but no bookwrights?

- Considering people from Poland are called Poles, why aren't those from Holland called Holes?

- In a fire drill you're told to walk in an orderly fashion, so why is the man in the emergency exit sign running?

- When forensic experts have to identify corpses by dental records, how do they know who their dentists are?

- If one synchronised swimmer drowns, do they all have to?

- How is it that Barry Manilow didn't write the song 'I Write The Songs'?

- Why do people add years onto their lives before they're 21 and from there on in start taking them off?

Witan Wisdom

- What's so fulfilling about fulfilment?

- Do people in Australia call the rest of the world 'Up Over'?

- Why is it that people who repair shoes are so good at cutting keys?

- Why do they never do research on whether research works?

- How young can you die of old age?

- Why do women never think they came out well in a photograph?

- Why do triangular-shaped sandwiches always taste better than rectangular ones?

- If truth is beauty, as Keats alleged, why aren't there more good-looking people in libraries?

- Do mothers cry at weddings because their daughters always insist on marrying men like their fathers?

- Why is it that the same people who laugh at fortune tellers take weather forecasters seriously?

- Considering ghosts can walk through doors, why don't they fall through floors?

- Why don't they make whole aeroplanes out of the same stuff as the black box?

- Considering Einstein believed time was relative, was he late for all his lectures?

- Do cemetery workers prefer the graveyard shift?

- How stupid was the guy who coined the term 'smart' bomb?

- If you're cross-eyed and have dyslexia, would you be able to see all right?

- If somebody with a multiple personality disorder threatens to kill themselves, would that be a hostage situation?

- Why do people I ask street directions from tell me to go around squares?

- Will there ever be a Christmas where they don't show The Sound Of Music on TV?

- Why don't efficiency experts go into business for themselves?

- Why is it that if you look as bad as your passport photo, you're probably not well enough to travel?

- Do masochists do it for kicks?

- Is crude oil much more harder to put manners on than the natural variety?

- Do policemen ever walk up and down the street thinking about how members of the public look younger than them?

- How is it that one careless match can start a forest fire, but it takes about ten to light a bbq?

Unlightenment

- Why do people who say they agree with something 'in principle' never do anything about it?

- How is it you always know you're in for a whopper of an insult when somebody says 'Don't take this personally'?

- Considering the high cost of living today, how do people in white collar jobs afford to have them laundered?

- How can I know what I think until I've heard what I've said?

- Why is society structured in such a way that when you finally find a way to make ends meet, they move the ends?

- If you want to order marijuana over the phone, should you press the hash key?

- If you try to fail but succeed instead, have you failed?

- Why don't teachers just call green blackboards greenboards?

- If carrots are good for your eyes, why do I see so many dead rabbits on the motorway?

- Why does the other queue always move faster until you leave your own one to go into it?

- Why will bank managers only give you a loan if you can prove to them that you don't need one?

- If Neil Armstrong bared his bum on the space trip in 1969, would that have been called 'mooning'?

- Can any horse go as fast as the money you bet on him?

- Why can't you buy inessential oils?

- Does anyone in the real world actually READ any of the books that win the Booker Prize?

- If women wear white on their wedding day to denote chastity, why do men wear black?

- Why do Americans spend Independence Day with other people?

- Do Krishnas go to the barber and say, 'Leave a little on the top'?

- Why do people say 'He wants to have his cake and eat it'? What good is a cake if you can't eat it?

- Is there a ring of debris round Uranus?

- Why do they call them Safety matches when you could burn a house down with them?

- What's the speed of dark?

- Why can you never put things back in a box the way they were before you opened it?

- What does the expression 'Between a rock and a hard place' mean? Is a rock not a hard place?

- Could a half-wit work part time for Intelligence?

- How do coroners get sacked? Who complains?

- If a woman speaks in the forest and there's no man to listen to her, is she still wrong?

- How have we put a man on the moon but still can't come up with a cafe tea-pot that doesn't leak?

- Do blondes prefer gentlemen?

- How do you go about studying for urine tests?

- At the Annual Sheepdog Trials, what do they do to the guilty ones?

- If ants are such good workers, how do they find time to go to all those picnics?

- If we came from apes, why are there still apes?

- If olive oil comes from olives and corn oil comes from corn, where does baby oil come from?

- If beauty is really truth, why don't more women get their hair done in the library?

- If flying is as safe as they tell us, why do planes land at 'terminals'?

- Are part-time band members semi-conductors?

- Why do people on the phone say 'I'll let you go' when what they really mean is they can't wait to get rid of you?

- Why is it that any food that doesn't make you put on weight tastes like crap?

- Why are there so many things to wonder about?

- Why do we call it a cargo if it's sent by ship, and a shipment if it comes by road?

- When signmakers go on strike, do they write anything on their strike placards?

- If a deaf person swears in sign language, does his mother wash his hands with soap?

Wild Wonderings

- Did anyone ever succeed in actually catching a wild goose?

- Do Playboy centrefolds grimace because of the pain of the staples?

- Did Monica Lewinsky blow it for Bill Clinton in politics?

- Now that Christmas is Xmas, should we not talk about Xians getting together for the Xening of a baby called Xtopher at Xchurch?

- Why do we call people magicians if they pull rabbits out of hats, but fools if they let cats out of bags?

- Why do people say they slept like a baby when babies wake up every two hours?

- Why do people pay to get to the top of skyscrapers and then put money into binoculars to see things on the ground?

- Why do people tell you secrets in confidence? If they can't keep it to themselves, why should you be expected to?

- How can they tell how many unreported crimes there are?

- Considering they call oranges 'orange', why don't they call apples 'red' or bananas 'yellow'?

- Why is it that a man who wasn't good enough to marry your daughter can still be the father of the smartest grandchild in the world?

- Why do people with 'Baby on Board' stickers in their cars continue to leave them there when baby isn't on board?

- Who do you complain to about the Complaints Department?

- Why do parents always take their children to the supermarket to smack them?

- Do parents tell their children the facts of life these days or is it the other way round?

- Why do people ask you if you slept badly when what they really mean is did you stay awake badly?

- Do some men call their wives 'duck' because of their big bills?

- Considering an orange is called an orange, why isn't a cabbage called a green?

- What kind of vulgarities are dockers using now that everyone else is using theirs?

- Would a male breast X-ray be called a Daddogram?

- Is it true that the greatest open spaces in the world can be found between people's ears?

- Why do people always say 'I hope you don't take this the wrong way' before they proceed to insult you?

- Why is it that when they say 'I'll let you know', they never do?

- Why is there always so much month left at the end of my money?

- Do astronauts ever dream of being little boys?

- If a little knowledge is a dangerous thing, how much do we need to be safe?

- When the Earl of Sandwich died, did they bury him between two other people?

- Is the hokey pokey really what it's all about?

- What bastard put the double 'er' in stutterer?

- Do transvestites leave the toilet seat up or down?

- Where do homeless people get off the bus?

- If you nail your toolshed shut, where do you put the hammer?

- Why is it that women who say they're free for the evening usually cost you a king's ransom?

- How do bellydancers get their jewels to stay in their navels as they wiggle?

- Why does the first pull on the cord always send the curtains in the wrong direction?

- Why do people never say 'It's only a game' when they've just won?

- How is it that all the people who advocate abortion have already been born?

- Why is the word 'big' smaller than 'little'?

- Did Procol Harum ever sing any other song besides 'A Whiter Shade of Pale'?

- Does hell have a smoking and non-smoking section?

- Why can women not put on make-up with their mouth closed?

- Which came first: the chicken or the egg? Or was it the rooster?

- Why don't producers of ballets just get taller dancers and then they wouldn't have to stand on their tiptoes?

- Why people who give you street directions tell you repeatedly that you 'can't miss it' – and you invariably do.

- Why can you write about murder, which is a crime, but not about sex, which isn't?

- Why, after 2,000 years on the planet, do men still believe women when they say they're ready?

- How can you have a 'civil' war?

- How can you sit on a damp towel for an hour and not realise it's wet till you stand up?

- Why do people fight for peace?

- Where do the things people do in airplane loos go to?

- Considering there's 7 days in a week and 52 weeks in a year, why doesn't 7 multiplied by 52 add up to 365.

- Why do people bother throwing boomerangs away?

- If we could move at the speed of light, would that mean we could lose our luggage before we left home?

- Why are there escalators to get you upstairs in department stores but only staircases to get you down again?

- If Maths teachers drive from A to B, do Algebra ones drive from X to Y?

- Why people make themselves sick with their first cigarette, and then get sick again after they give them up.

Brainiac Arrest

- Why does glue not stick to the container it comes in?

- Do blind Eskimos have seeing-eye sledge dogs?

- Why, since it's usually involved with self-denial, isn't willpower called won't power?

- Will Pamela Anderson's film career ever amount to anything more than a storm in a C-cup?

- Are men who call women broads narrow-minded?

- Why is it that, no matter how long you boil the meat in a TV dinner, it still tastes like leather?

- How did a fool and his money get together in the first place?

- If a bee was crossed with a cow, would the land flow with milk and honey?

- Why, when you get out of the bath to answer the phone, is it invariably a wrong number?

- Since babies born out of wedlock are called 'love children', does this mean legitimate babies come from hate?

- Why does junk mail never get lost?

- Why do computer screens always jump up and down when you see them on TV?

- Did the Invisible Man ever play Hide and Seek?

- Why does the first item on an airport conveyor belt never seem to belong to anyone?

- Why do parents who tell children to behave like grown-ups always sound like children themselves when they're saying it?

- Considering glue comes from horses, why don't they feel sticky?

- Why do teachers tell you to look up words in dictionaries that you can't spell. Where would you start?

- How is it that the less material there is in a bikini, the more it costs?

- Why are soccer players at touchlines, in equatorial venues described as 'warming up'?

- Do flashers refer to their genitals as public parts?

- Where do people who live at the seaside go on their holidays?

- Why does the Psychic Network need a phone number?

- Why is filling in a form and filling one out the same thing?

- Would a fly without wings be called a walk?

- Why is there always one ice cube that refuses to pop out of the tray?

- If crime fighters fight crime and fire fighters fight fire, what do freedom fighters fight?

- Why are people never too busy to tell you how busy they are?

- If it wasn't for Venetian blinds would it be curtains for all of us?

- What if there were no hypotheses?

- If women need to feel loved before they can have sex, and men need to have sex before they can love, how does anything get started?

- If you order Stryofoam, what do they wrap it in?

- If you got fired from your job at the unemployment office, could you go back the next day to sign on?

- Why is it that when the doorbell rings, the dog always thinks it's for him?

- Why do lifts stop at floors where there are no people waiting to get on?

- Will Martin Scorsese ever make a film bad enough to win an Oscar?

- Considering nobody knows when anyone is going to die, how can we ever say someone died prematurely?

- Is artificial intelligence a match for natural stupidity?

- Do Irish people wear two condoms to be sure, to be sure?

- What would happen if you got half scared to death twice?

- Why isn't there mouse-flavoured cat food?

- Do blondes have more fun because they're easier to find in the dark?

- When a building is finished, shouldn't it be called a built?

- Why does nobody gossip about other people's secret virtues?

- Do surgeons wear masks in case anything goes wrong?

- Could you use a handkerchief dress to blow your nose?

- If a lot of Shakespeares started fiddling around with typewriters for a thousand years, would they eventually write a monkey?

- What would you send to a sick florist?

- If talk is cheap, why are my phone bills always so high?

- Why can people never realise that the batteries on remote controls do actually run out eventually?

- Why do so many neighbours suffer from interferiority complexes?

- Is Guilt the Irish G-spot?

- If a woman falls at a man's feet nowadays, is it a sign he has dirty socks?

- Is the greatest pleasure in life to do good by stealth and have it discovered by accident?

- Why do people use answering machines to screen calls and then get 'Call Waiting' so they won't miss hearing from someone they didn't want to talk to in the first place?

- Why are boxing rings square?

- Do failed magicians become disillusioned?

- If absolute power corrupts absolutely, does absolute powerlessness then make you more pure?

And finally...

- Is the end of a book a 'book end'?

EPILOG

Now that you have completed this book, before you log off completely, you need to find another 'toilet-time' book before your next 'logging out' session.

All books by Jamien Bailey (Amazon/Jamien Bailey) are toilet friendly tomes.

If you read 5 pages of a book with an average of 300 pages (and if you poo once a day) then you will read 6 books a year that you would otherwise not have read. Never underestimate the entertainment value of 'Logging Out'.

Happy logging!

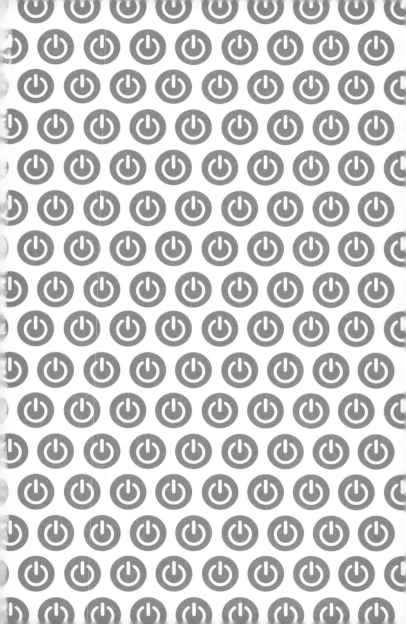

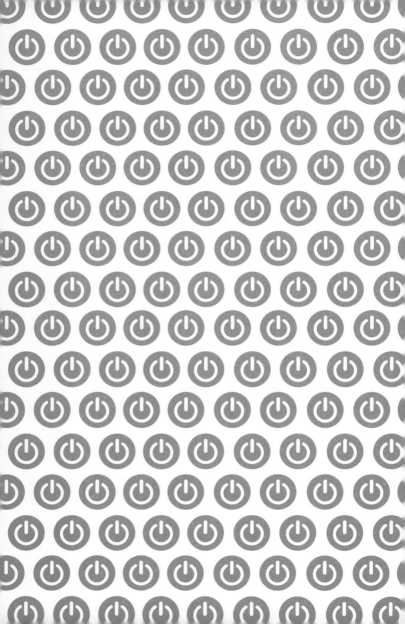